The Broadsheet Book
of Unspecified Things
that look like Ireland

BROADSHEET

Book of Unspecified

Things

that look like

Ireland

Edited by
Aidan Coughlan

NEW ISLAND

THE BROADSHEET BOOK OF UNSPECIFIED
THINGS THAT LOOK LIKE IRELAND
First published 2013 by New Island
2 Brookside
Dundrum Road
Dublin 14
www.newisland.ie

PRINT ISBN: 978-1-84840-253-9
EPUB ISBN: 978-1-84840-254-6
MOBI ISBN: 978-1-84840-255-3

British Library Cataloguing Data. A CIP catalogue record for this book is
available from the British Library

Typeset by Aidan Coughlan
Cover design by Aidan Coughlan and James M Chimney
Cover image by Lynn Donovan
Back illustration by Annie West
Printed by Bell & Bain Limited, Glasgow

New Island received financial assistance from The Arts Council
(An Comhairle Ealaíon), Dublin, Ireland

10 9 8 7 6 5 4 3 2 1

Thank You

A book like this doesn't come together without goodwill and assistance aplenty, so a few words of thanks are in order from all of us at Broadsheet Towers.

To Bodger, Ewok, Chompsky, Nat King Coleslaw, James M Chimney, John Moynes, Emily O'Callaghan, Karl Monaghan, Aaron McAllorum, Dominic Hyde, Niall Murphy, Susie Phillips, Gavan Titley, DelBoy, Sam Dunne, Lars Biscuits, Not Pancho, Michael Le Cool, Ciaran Le Cool, Sarah E Leahy and John 'Preposterous' Ryan – all of whom have helped bring this project to life.

To Eoin Purcell at New Island, who believed and took a punt; to Elaine Herbert, who helped separate the wheat from the Ireland-shaped wheat.

To other assorted helpers: Aongus Collins, Annie West, Sinéad Keogh, Lynn Donovan, Louise Roe, all at Aware, Ronan Lyons and Fod.

And most of all: to everyone who contributed to this ongoing, weird and wonderful project. Cheers!

Aidan: I'll add to that a special thanks to my wonderful girlfriend Rachel, who kept sound my sanity (and baked me cookies) while I struggled to stay afloat in a sea of island-shaped objects. And of course, Frank, Debs, Elle and Jean; my bizarre, unique and fantastic family. Sure where would ye get it.

A Word
From Aware

The *Broadsheet Book of Unspecified Things That Look Like Ireland* is a clever and humorous approach to seeing Ireland differently. *Aware* is delighted and very appreciative that some of the proceeds of this book are going to support the work which *Aware* does in helping people see depression differently.

Details of the various services which *Aware* provides are available on the website, aware.ie, and include the Helpline, Support Groups and email support services as well as a Life-Skills programme and the 'Beat the Blues' programme which is aimed at Senior Cycle secondary students.

While the increase in emigration may cause many families additional pressures, *The Broadsheet Book of Unspecified Things That Look Like Ireland* remind us to stand back, look at things differently and smile.

We wish the book every success,

Dr Claire Hayes,
Clinical Director, *Aware*

Contents

← Previous

Next →

The Hedge That Looks Like Ireland

1:02 pm October 4, 2011 Ewok

"On the road between Goleen and Barleycove, West Cork." (Diarmaid Frain)

Introduction

It happened on a Tuesday in October, 2011. Diarmaid Frain came across a hedge in West Cork and, upon noticing its resemblence to the Emerald Isle, emailed it to Broadsheet HQ. It was posted to the site shortly after 1pm that day, and received a total of 12 comments over the following nine hours and 15 minutes.

That same very evening, seven men and women lined up in front of Vincent Browne for a debate on TV3. The presidential election was to take place in three weeks' time, and each candidate had a clear case to state: that they, moreso than their opponents or any other person, could be the best representation of our small nation both at home and overseas.

What they could not have known was that a process had already taken form that would, eventually, render their most earnest efforts in vain; a process that would define us in terms far clearer and more truthful than any man-made office ever could.

This book does not aim to provide a chronological guide to that progress, but simply to show us how far we have truly come.

From Derry to Dungarvan, from Bray to Ballina, and from Sydney to Seattle, Unspecified Things That Look Like Ireland has become the force that shows us, and reminds us, what it is to be of this land.

In October of 2011, we saw a hedge; now we see an entire nation.

And of that, we must be proud.

Aidan Coughlan

The Edible Section

The top of a lovely cheese cake,
And a thick, freshly fried fillet steak,
Both resemble our land,
As do ham, schnitzels and,
Even a Special K flake.

John Moynes (1713-1800)

The orange peel (with contour lines) that looks like Ireland.

Danielle Martin

The beans and toast that look like Great Britain and Ireland

Fergal Davey

The delicious homemade crisps that look like Ireland

Ferg Flannery

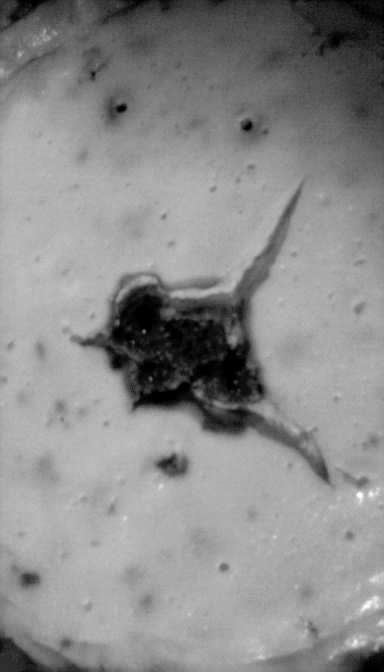

The raspberry bit of a raspberry cheesecake that looks like Ireland

Louise Donlon

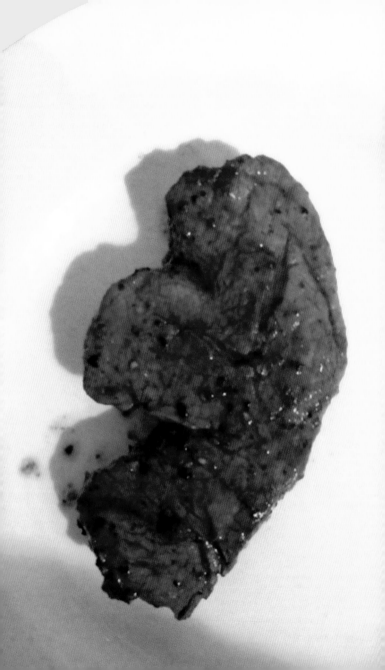

The first steak of many that look like Ireland

Christmas was fast approaching, my wife Eva and I decided to splash out and get two fillet steaks for dinner. On entering the pan the steaks looked quite different. One a perfect circle reminiscent of a delicious 'hockey puck' the other, as it sizzled began to transform into the shape you see here: the Emerald Isle!

It can only be the gods sending the steak home for The Gathering – or a clear message that the steak was meant for me, as I am Irish! I quickly plated it up and managed to get a photo. Then....it disappeared! With chips...

Barry Dignam

The cut bread in Canada that
(now) looks like Ireland.

Sean Connolly

A slice of my mother's homemade soda bread that looks like Ireland

After another long year slaving over a hot keyboard in London, I was at home at my parents place in Limerick for Christmas. Any time I'm at home I try to deanglicise myself by eating as much Irish grub as I can. On this occasion, my mum had baked some soda bread. Perfect! The loaf didn't look at all unusual when I approached it with the bread knife.

As I began to slice through the bread, I could almost sense the impending magic. The freshly sliced piece of bread keeled over on its side, revealing its glorious hibernian structure for all to see. A month later I'm now back at my desk in London dreaming of Ireland shaped soda-bread when I should be working.

Martin Burke

My boyfriend's steak that looks like Ireland

Lorna Byrne

The toast that looks like Ireland (with chocolate spread on top)

Evan

The bit of butter in a baking bowl that looks like Ireland

Adam Baker

The ginger root that looks like a mummified Ireland

Mice Hell

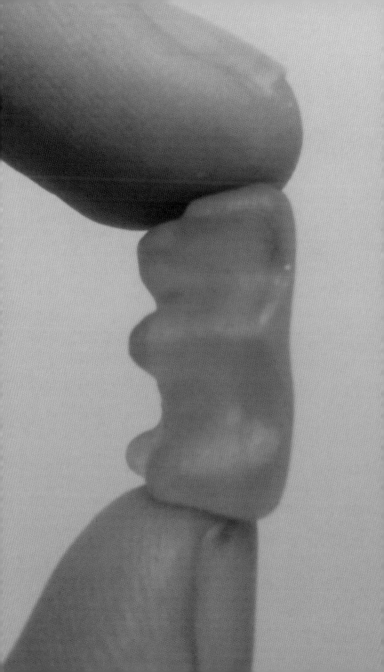

The sweet that, like all green gummy bears, looks like Ireland

So there I was, tucking into my daily bowl of jellies (the breakfast of champions) and somewhere between a sour snake and milk teeth I spotted the little green bear and to my astonishment, it looked *exactly* like Ireland!

I managed to stave off my appetite for confectionery for a few moments while I took a snap to show all my friends – now, not only do I regret eating the jelly-Éire but also not having cleaned my grubby fingernails.

Seán Mullen

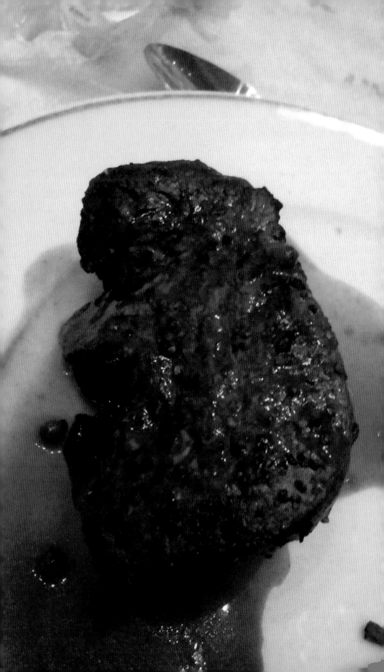

The steak at a friend's wedding that looks like Ireland

Paddy O'Connor

The thing that looks like Ireland,
but about which there is
no point crying

Alaisia Kelly

The Dalkey hash brown that looks like Ireland

Kevin O'Farrell

The Special K flake that looks like Ireland

Suzanne Crotty

My breakfast that looks like Ireland (with a tail)

Sonja Eisenberg

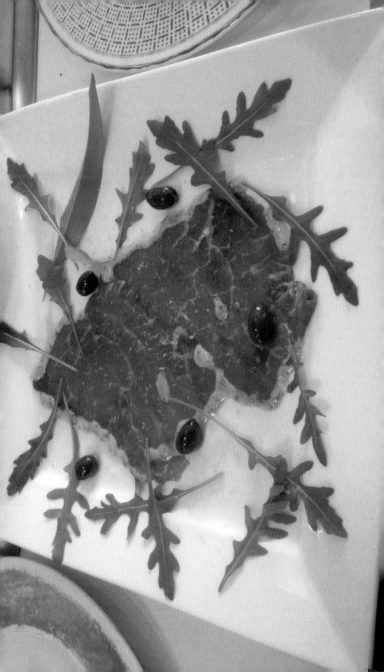

The beef carpaccio that looks like Ireland

Lisa Devlin

The schnitzel in Stockholm that looks like Ireland

I have been living outside Ireland for 4 years and have a reputation in work for being over patriotic ('Irish, not British' catchphrase). On a business trip to Stockholm I was in a restaurant with colleagues.

When the waitress served my meal (Veal Schnitzel) I immediately proclaimed: "My schnitzel looks like Ireland!" The confusion on my colleagues' faces indicated I needed to explain it wasn't a euphemism.

I pointed at the plate and said "This schnitzel looks like Ireland". Thankfully they all agreed, and it wasn't just me "being so Irish" to think it. Ireland tasted good, as you would expect.

Shane Kerr

My brother's wanton disregard for eggs that looks like Ireland

Caoimhe Lavelle

The froth in my Bangkok beer that looks like Ireland

Gavan Timlin

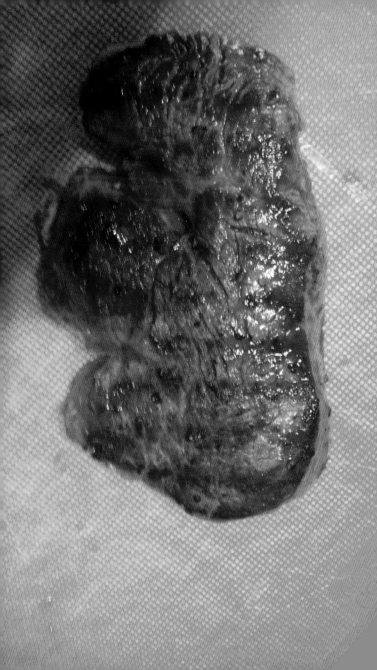

Another steak that looks like Ireland

Brendan Howard

The orange panna cotta that
looks like Ireland.

Johnny Cox

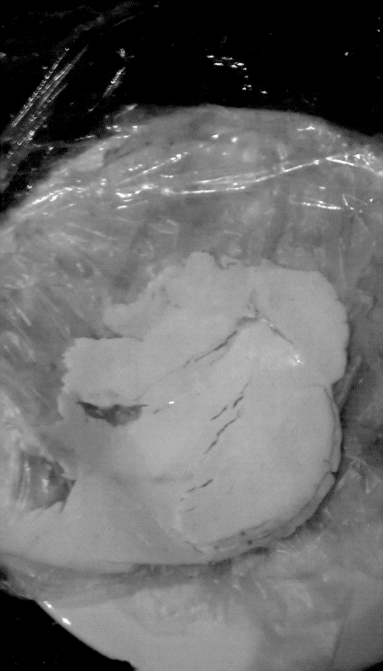

The (genuinely, randomly torn-in-half-to-make-a-sandwich) slice of turkey that looks like Ireland

Suzanne Crotty

The Duncan Stewart Suite

And now for a handful of pics,
Of things made from mortar and bricks,
And also some quaint,
Pictures of peeling paint
To give you your Ireland-shaped fix.

John Moynes (1810-1898)

The plastered wall that looks like Ireland

Brian McGuinness

The side of a building in Sienna that looks like Ireland

Margaret Lyons

The patch of wall in Dublin,
where the paint peeled away due
to a leak, that now looks like
Ireland (with a discoloured North)

Lisa Keane

The glue left over from a poster in Andorra that looks like Ireland

Aran Brazil

The paint anomaly that looks like Ireland (with continental shelf)

Sam Scriven

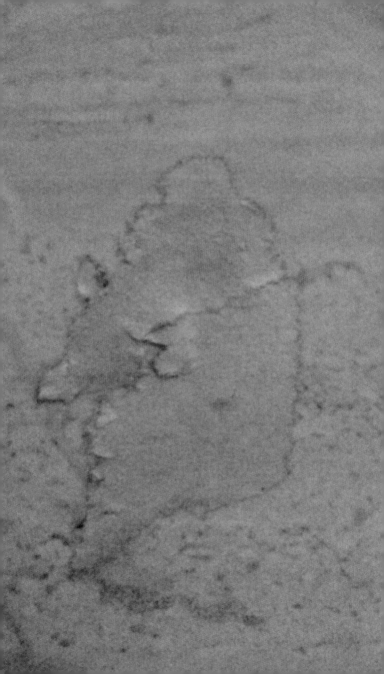

The stain on a wall that looks like Ireland

Paddy O'Connor

The wood grain that looks like a widened Ireland

Des Moriarty

Interlude:
An Economist's View

As Irishmen and women, we all know that 2013, as the year of the Blathering, is a crossroads for the country. We are where we are and have been there for a good few years now. We might not be where we were in the good old days, but we're somewhere anyway – and that's a start.

But going forward, this book contains a very stark warning for Ireland. Until now, we have traded on our uniqueness. This important book, however, tells us that we are not alone. Ireland faces competition from all over the world. Dozens of things, from lumps of pyrite in D.C., to puddles in Auckland, and even orange panna cottas, have stripped us of the notion that we were in some way special in this globalised world.

The array of other Irelands – from dead pigeons hanging off trees to jelly beans, from chipped flower pots to juicy steaks – are effectively a wave of new supply to the global Éire market. All good economists have catchy names for these things, so I am going to call this the Ryanair effect. As we all know, the emergence of Michael O'Leary on to the air travel market in the 1990s spelled the end for £500-return flights to London.

What we are seeing in this book is a wave of Michael O'Learys, all chipping away at our heretofore unique selling point. Why would OmniCorp set up their European & Middle East HQ in Ireland when

The piece of fluff that looks like Ireland, by economist Ronan Lyons

they could set it up instead in a volcanic ash plume that looks really like Ireland instead?

So, just like the emergence of China on to the world economy or the fall of the Berlin Wall, the ramifications of Unspecified Things That Look Like Ireland for the Irish economy, the Irish society, indeed the Irish psyche, will be profound.

As we are often told, we live in the age of the knowledge economy, the smart economy. It would not be smart to ignore the knowledge in this book. We are not alone.

Ronan Lyons
Daft Economist

The
Uncategorisables

Here are the things miscellaneous,
Some odd, and some downright extraneous,
Though if truth be told,
Some of these are quite old,
While others are contemporaneous.

John Moynes (1822-1914)

The central column of Berlin's Weltzeituhr that should, but doesn't, look like Ireland

Conor Horgan

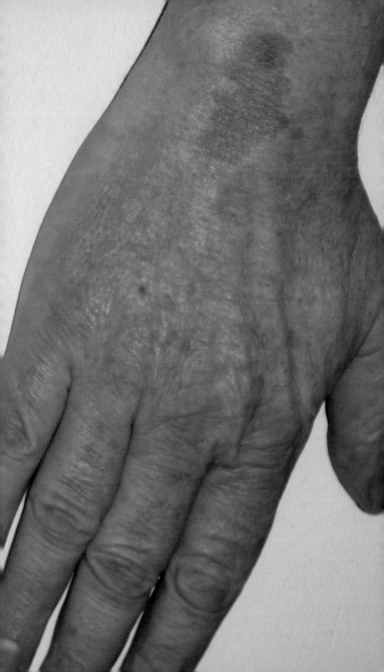

The birthmark on a person born on St Patrick's Day that looks like Ireland

Patrick McHugh

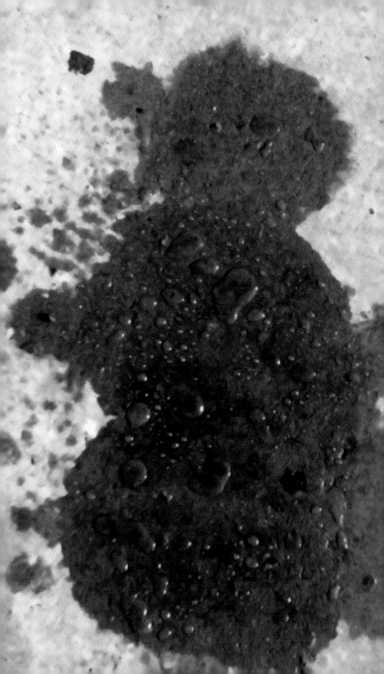

The diesel spill in Inis Meáin that looks like Ireland

Deano Murray

The who-knows-what on the ground in Roscommon that looks like Ireland

Rob Collins

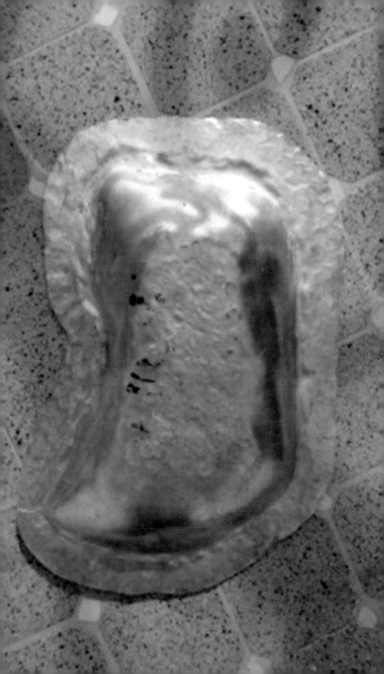

The ashtray made by my American brother-in-law that looks like Ireland

Andrew Moore

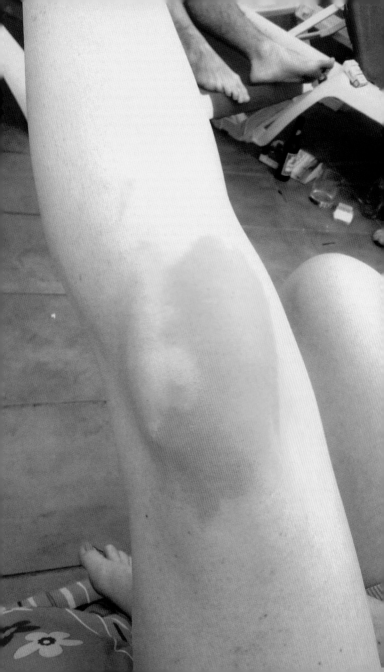

The sunburn on my friend Kat's knee that looks like Ireland

Cormac Ó Conaire

The rock scum in Inis Oirr that looks like Ireland

Lucy Banks

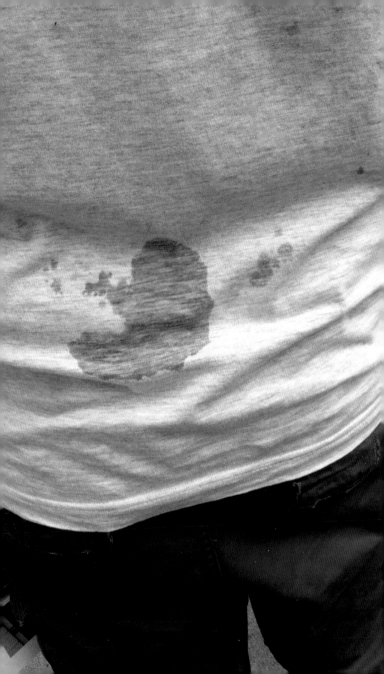

The sweat patch in Ljubljana that looks like Ireland

Mike O'Dell

The pile of mud in Hyde Park that looks like Ireland

Deirdre Power

The last of my makeup that looks like Ireland

Jill O'Lone

The earrings in a New York jewellery store that look like Ireland

Clare Dunne

BROADSHEET

The Jay Leno that looks like Ireland

Diane Sabba

The mark on a speedbump that looks like Ireland

Mark Sugrue

The pothole in the African Museum Park, Brussels, that looks like Ireland

Brian O'Connell

The piece of pub candle wax in Brighton that looks like Ireland

Cathy McHugh

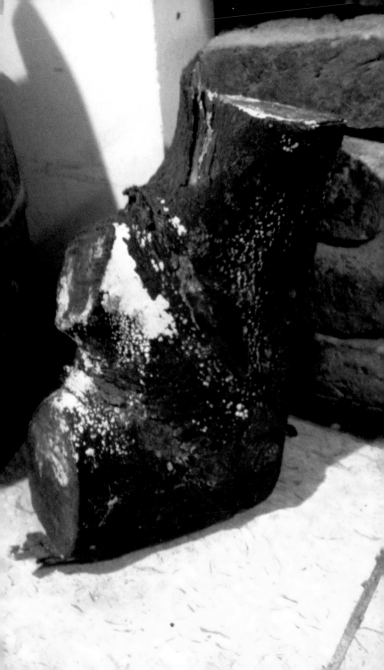

The piece of firewood that looks like Ireland

James Tuomey

The floating rubbish on the Liffey that looks like Ireland

It was late February 2009, and the financial crisis was still fairly new and frightening. I was in my final year in Trinity, preparing to graduate into a very uncertain economy. I left my student room on campus and went out for an early morning run. I ran down the south quays and came to the new developments, enormous empty office blocks with tape still stuck on the windows.

Then I came to the place where the development abruptly stopped. The pavement ended, and the flashy buildings gave way to scrub land. Struck, I stopped running and explored this spit of wasteland, sticking out into the Liffey, scraggy grass littered with the odd bit of twisted metal and a leaking hosepipe.

I turned around and began to run back towards Trinity, and crossed over the Sean O'Casey bridge to do the journey back on the North Quays. That's when I spotted it. The rubbish floating in the Liffey that looked like Ireland. It was all so poetically apt.

Naomi O'Leary

BROADSHEET

The damp patch in Sandymount that looks like Ireland

Gareth Heffernan

The Pasadena car park puddle that looks like Ireland

Dan McNamee / Rachel Wiseman

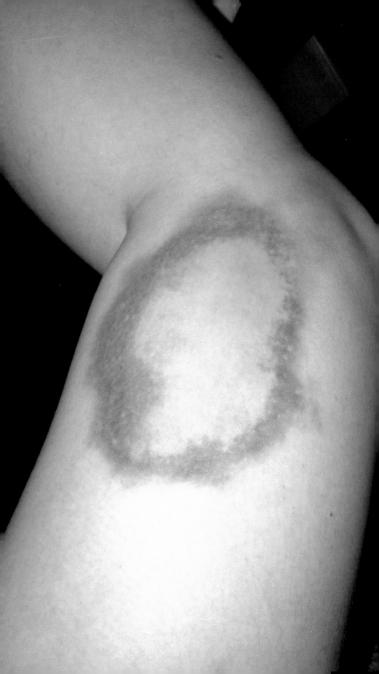

The bruise from when I came off my scooter that looks like Ireland

I got my bruise in November 2012 I came off my scooter on the way to work on a rainy Tuesday morning, I live in Bermuda so scooters are the easiest and cheapest way to get around, I got a bit of flack for having one on the comments on Broadsheet!

I went to a wedding in England about a week and a half later and it was there I saw the bruisae had changed shape and now looked like home! I asked my boyfriend what he thought and he recognised it instantly, my sisters - not so quick! I bruise like a peach and have had some impressive shapes and colours in my time but this one was definitely my best work.

Rachel

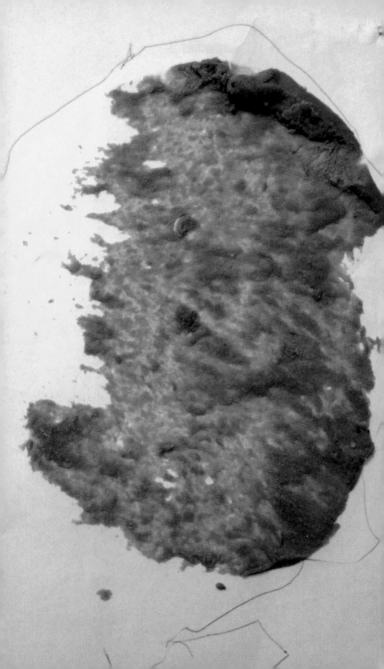

The remains of some playdough,
which my four-year-old son stuck
to a page, that looks like Ireland

Jennifer Cassidy

The Chicken
Nugget Section

The chicken, a feathery bird,
Can be chopped up and battered and stirred,
In hot boiling oil.
The result of this toil,
Looks like Ireland each time, how absurd!

John Moynes (1723-1815)

Brendan Foley

Noreen Healy

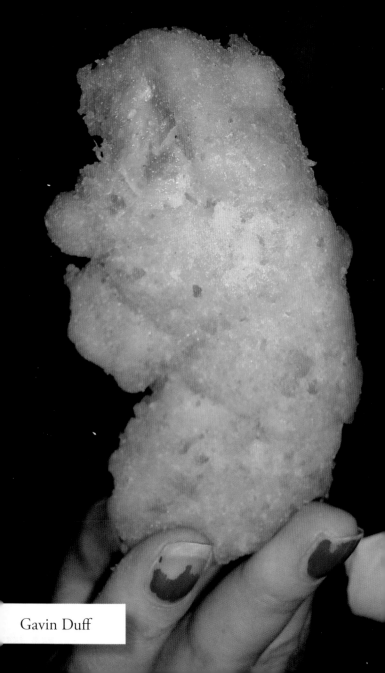

Gavin Duff

Seán A Conneely

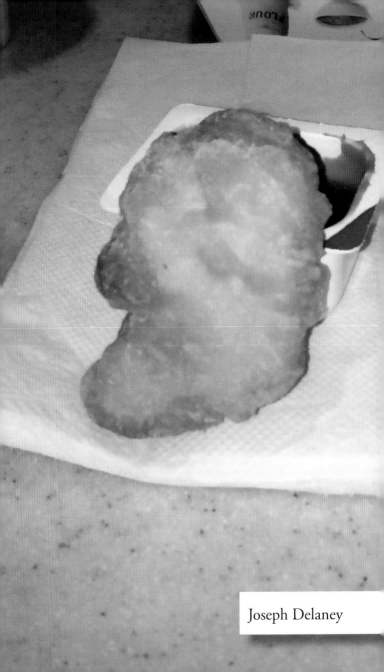

Joseph Delaney

Louise Morris

Hairy McBoon

The Ptolemy Section

A scone, or a puddle of ale,
Might resemble the land of the Gael.
Or it mightn't, you see,
For in all honesty,
The following items all fail.

John Moynes (1910-1942)

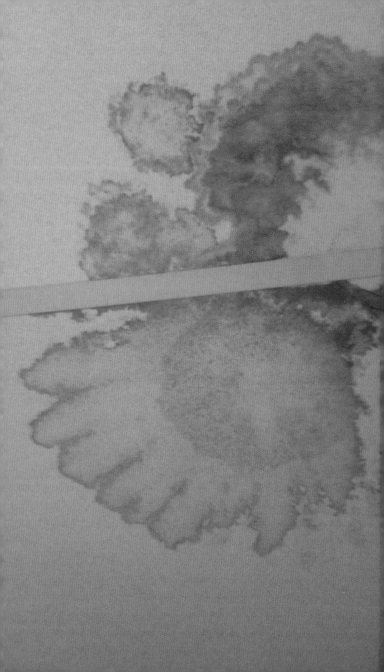

The damp spot on the office ceiling that looks like Ireland

Dermot Donovan

The broken window, from when
my bro 'had' to get his passport
for a trip to the 'Dam at New Year,
that kinda looks like Ireland

Conor McKeogh

The sideways cloud that kinda looks like Ireland

Sheila Flynn

The sign on a Cologne hairdresser that looks like Ireland

Marcel Krueger

The 7-Up spill that looks like Ireland

Carlosfandango

The cloud in Sydney that looks like Ireland

Niamh Conlon

The piece of Blu-Tac that looks like Ireland

Stephen Doyle

By Alan Pollock

Interlude:
Sconegate Revisited

In late 2012, Broadsheet's much-loved 'Unspecified Things That Look Like Ireland' feature caused widespread controversy, when it was found that one of the featured images did not look like Ireland at all. This was the website's response.

In the fast paced world of modern media, it is inevitable that mistakes will be made.

Lord Justice Leveson's report into the British media paints a grim picture of corruption, bullying, crime and an entire industry divorced from the very concept of morality.

However, sometimes the very speed of online publishing causes mistakes to be made innocently. While no website can be wholly free from error, all must correct their own mistakes, and must apologise in public for them.

An internal investigation has concluded that on December 4, Ewok posted a picture of a scone which, it was claimed, looked like Ireland. The scone did not, in fact, look like Ireland.

Here at *Broadsheet* we are proud of our long-standing commitment to highlighting unspecified things that look recognisably like Ireland. We apologise for the annoyance and any navigational errors caused by our cartographically-inaccurate bun.

The Natural
Selection

If you notice an Ireland-shaped cloud,
Or a tree, as they're also allowed,
Or a bush, or you might,
Spot some chalcopyrite,
Well, send it it to us and feel proud.

John Moynes (1210-1297)

The puddle in Mayo that looks like Ireland

Garrett Walsh

The lake in Three Castles Head, Co Cork, that looks like Ireland

Claire Brady

The smoke plume from an erupting New Zealand volcano that looks like Ireland

Lynn Donovan

The dead pigeon, hanging in a field, that looks like Ireland

Tadhg O'Halloran

The cloud in Rathgar, Co Dublin, that looks like Ireland

It was a wonderful, sunny day in May 2009, myself and a friend were basking in the rare Irish summer rays. We remarked that, for all the shapes that clouds are, they rarely resemble anything, unless you dropped some LSD.

Our imaginations alone were not free enough to form anything recognisable and we gave up. However, moments later, Ireland drifted into view in all its glory.

WhaddayaNuts!

The upstanding hedge that looks like Ireland

Peter Glavey

The side of the University of Music and Performing Arts in Vienna that looks like Ireland

Gavan Flinter

The moss that looks like Ireland

I spotted this while walking through the undergrowth on a little island on Lake Winnipesaukee, New Hampshire, during the summer of 2008. I went up north with some friends as a brief espape from buzzing NYC and stayed in my friend Matt's parents' idyllic waterside cabin on another island of the lake archipelago.

We felt like natives exploring the wilderness... until we came back to reality with my excited exclamation that I found a lump of moss that looked like Ireland.

Nóirín Ní Earcáin

Chalcopyrite
Chalcopyrite

Galena

The block of chalcopyrite in Ontario that looks like Ireland

David Neary

The tree in Kensington Gardens, London, that looks like Ireland

I was on the dole at the time after college for months and had flown expensively to London for an interview. The interview itself was a complete disaster; it was one of those occasions where you can't wait to get out of the place and the baking heat wasn't providing much solace once outside.

Rather than sight-seeing and soaking up a bit of culture I, demoralised as I was at the time with another week's dole-money wasted on an interview, just wanted to go to a park and have a snooze and maybe even get a consolatory ice-cream.

When I woke from my long, restorative Kensington snooze my eyes opened only to see Ireland in the branches overhead. I got a job not that long after that – so maybe there was a bit of luck in it.

Therese O'Donoghue

La Rioja, Spain

Pyrite
· · · · ·
FeS₂
Tasna, Potosí, Bolivia

The fool's gold (pyrite) in Washington, DC, that looks like Ireland

Tom Dillon

The puddle on Beartra beach in Westport, Co Mayo, that looks like Ireland

Emmett Keane

The tree at Electric Picnic that looks like Ireland

This was taken at the 2007 festival. Some of our friends had gone off to see Primal Scream but me and my wife to be Aileen slipped into Damien Dempsey at the Crawdaddy tent. It was our first time seeing him live and he LIFTED the roof off the place.

Anyway we came out after the gig, the crowd was still singing 'It's All Good' in the background, and we saw this tree. Loads of other heads were standing around looking at it, so we just took a photo.

Ruairi Carroll

The cloud on the N5 that looks like Ireland

Niall Mullally

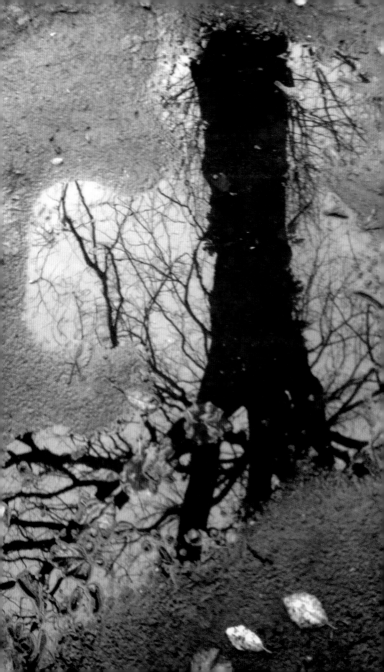

The autumnal puddle that looks like Ireland

Dermot Donovan

A pothole on the Caribbean island of Culebra, off the coast of Puerto Rico, that looks like Ireland

When visiting a friend in Puerto Rico we took the opportunity to spend a few nights in the Culebra, whose Flamenco Beach is rated amongst one of the best beaches in the world. Setting off for an early morning snorkel we came across this pothole and couldn't resist taking a snap – the irony of an Ireland-shaped pothole was too good to pass by. That much we agreed on.

What we haven't agreed on since its new-found notoriety is who was the photographer. The moral of the story? Always make sure there are people in your holiday photos!

Carina and Diarmaid Brophy

www.broadsheet.ie